WOLVERHAMPTON'S RAILWAYS IN COLOUR

BY SIMON DEWEY

First Published in 2010 by Simon Dewey, 49 Tyninghame Avenue, Tettenhall, Wolverhampton WV6 9PP on behalf of the Severn Valley Railway (Wolverhampton Branch)

All distribution enquiries should be addressed to the publisher.

Printed by Amadeus Press, Ezra House, West 26 Business Park, Cleckheaton, West Yorkshire, BD19 4TQ.
Tel: (01274) 863210. E-mail: info@amadeuspress.co.uk.
Website: www.amadeuspress.co.uk

ISBN 978-0-9565797-0-6

Above: GWR "Castle" 7014 "Caerhays Castle", alongside the coaling stage at its then home shed of Stafford Road in mid-1963 awaiting coaling. The engine is fitted with a double chimney and is one of a number of the class provided with an additional reservoir feeding the mechanical lubricator on the side of the smokebox. On closure of Stafford Road in September 1963, 7014 was transferred to Oxley shed from where it was withdrawn in February 1965.

Front cover: "Britannia" Pacific No 70045 "Lord Rowallan" departs from Wolverhampton Low Level station and below Sun Street bridge towards the tunnel with a summer Saturday express to Portsmouth in 1965 during the short period of its allocation to Oxley shed between June and September of that year. Electrification of the High Level line is proceeding, with gantries in place but as yet no wiring. The new High Level signal box, commissioned on 18th August 1964, is visible above Sun Street bridge and below St Peter's church tower, with the Chubb lock building to its right. J.N.Miller's flour and provender mill and the Low Level stationmaster's house, obscured by the engine's exhaust, are partially visible above 70045's tender. The lines in the foreground lead up to connect to the Midland Railway line at Heath Town Junction.   *John Bucknall*

Back cover: For several years following opening of the rebuilt High Level station and commencement of electrified services in March 1967, locomotives were stabled on the sidings at the eastern side of Wolverhampton station (the suffix "High Level" was dropped during 1973) on what is now the site of Platform 4. Class 87 87 005 "City of London" and Class 85 85 003 are seen parked in 1984.   *Simon Dewey*

Foreword by Pete Waterman

Quite why a kid from Coventry should become so fascinated with Wolverhampton and the Black Country I have no idea save perhaps that although Coventry has lots of industry, Wolverhampton always seemed to me to have so much more.

I knew really after visiting Stafford Road Works in the mid 1950's (courtesy of a hole in the fence, and in the company of my best mate Tommy) that there was really only one place where I wanted to work when I left school in 1963! To me, Wolverhampton, Oxley and Bushbury were magical places and as long as the pocket money was forthcoming, most Saturdays found me on my way to Wolverhampton and, other than Leamington Spa and Rugby, I certainly spent more time spotting these locations than anywhere else. The journey from Snow Hill to Wolverhampton was in itself a fantastic experience and Snow Hill Station was just unbelievable but there was something extra special about Wolverhampton Low Level. Given my reputation, it might surprise you to learn that I very rarely went to the ex LNWR station and this was because I found the end of the platform on Low Level so entertaining and so rewarding that I was always fully occupied.

About lunchtime, we would always nip onto the canal side, walk down to Stafford Road and then go in either via the canal, crossing the lock gates or by walking down Stafford Road and trying to nip round the back! However, if a shilling was in your pocket, the best way was on the DMU to Dunstall Park, then while everyone else was walking off the station to the Stafford Road, you'd walk around the other way and nip down the lane that led to the shed, which was probably breaking every rule but I can honestly say that I never had any trouble doing this.

By the time I got to know the main shed at Wolverhampton it was in a pretty run down state but the lines of Castles, Counties and Kings more than made up for the dilapidation. Walking out of the back of the shed, up the steps and across the barrow crossing into the Stafford Road Works was an amazing experience because the place was littered with bits and pieces of steam locomotives - I thought I'd died and gone to Heaven!

Today, I can categorically say that I was hugely influenced by all that I saw at that young age and that this manifests itself today in the work that we do on repairing steam engines in our workshops. So to Wolverhampton I say "thank you for the inspiration".

This book is about those locations and for all those who missed them, you missed an amazing era - even the muck had a magical appeal! I consider myself very lucky to still have friends from all those years ago who spotted in the Wolverhampton area. My Leamington Spa layout allows me to indulge myself and be transported back to those amazing lazy summer days of the 1950's when most of the traffic I saw at Leamington Spa would have come from Stafford Road, Oxley or Tyseley.

Enjoy the book, it records an era that I'm sure will never be seen again - to which some may say, 'Thank God!' - but for me, it's with a sense of privilege that I'll cherish those memories. *Pete Waterman, March 2010*

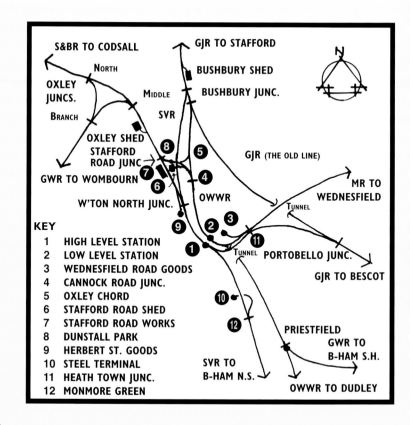

KEY
1. HIGH LEVEL STATION
2. LOW LEVEL STATION
3. WEDNESFIELD ROAD GOODS
4. CANNOCK ROAD JUNC.
5. OXLEY CHORD
6. STAFFORD ROAD SHED
7. STAFFORD ROAD WORKS
8. DUNSTALL PARK
9. HERBERT ST. GOODS
10. STEEL TERMINAL
11. HEATH TOWN JUNC.
12. MONMORE GREEN

Introduction

Wolverhampton was a significant railway centre for over 100 years from the 1850's to the 1960's.

The first railway to reach the town (as it was then), the Grand Junction Railway, (GJR) arrived in 1837 passing to the east from Bushbury via Heath Town towards Willenhall, Wolverhampton's first station being located at Heath Town (Wednesfield Heath). The town council of the day had been suspicious of the new form of transport and unwilling to permit its passage though the centre of the town.

In 1846 the GJR merged with the London & Birmingham Railway to create the London & North Western Railway (LNWR), the country's first trunk railway and backbone of the present-day West Coast main line.

The first line to pass through the centre of the town was the Birmingham, Wolverhampton & Stour Valley Railway, (SVR) sanctioned in 1846, leased to the LNWR in 1847 and ultimately opened in 1852, running from Bushbury where it connected to the GJR just south of Bushbury Lane bridge, thence across a lengthy viaduct rising across the Smestow valley to the station that was to become High Level but was originally known as Queen Street station. The line continued south via Tipton, Dudley Port and Oldbury to Navigation Street, Birmingham.

In 1849 the Shrewsbury & Birmingham Railway (S&BR) was opened, entering Wolverhampton from the northwest over Oxley viaduct and aiming to connect to the SVR to proceed over SVR metals to Birmingham but opening to a temporary station just north of Wednesfield Road and near Broad Street canal basin pending connection to the yet to be completed SVR.

The fundamental form of the town's railways for the next century became settled in 1854 with the Oxford, Worcester & Wolverhampton Railway (OWWR) entering from Priestfield and extending northwards through what became Low Level station and on to connect to the GJR/LNWR at Bushbury. In conjunction with the arrival of the OWWR, the Great Western Railway (GWR) also commenced running into the town from Birmingham, their Birmingham, Wolverhampton & Dudley Railway (BW&D) joining the OWWR at Priestfield.

Other than the GWR's branch line to Wombourn (always spelt without the 'e' by the GWR) opened in 1925, the final railway connection into the town, from the Walsall direction, arrived in 1872 with the completion of the Wolverhampton & Walsall Railway, vested with the LNWR but sold in 1876 to the Midland Railway (MR) who constructed their Wednesfield Road Goods Depot between 1878 and 1881. A spur from this line at Heath Town to the LNWR at Portobello was built in 1881.

The S&BR and OWWR were acquired by the GWR in 1854 and 1863 respectively who firmly established themselves in Wolverhampton with their Low Level station, engine sheds at Stafford Road and Oxley, locomotive works at Stafford Road, marshalling yards at Oxley and goods depots at Victoria Basin (subsequently Herbert Street) and Monmore Green.

On the Grouping of the railways in 1923 the GWR retained its title but the LNWR and MR became part of the London Midland & Scottish Railway (LMS).

By comparison with that of the GWR, the impact of the LMS constituents on the town was quite limited yet has proved the more enduring, most of the GWR's establishments and lines being progressively closed from 1962 onwards. Of those remaining, Oxley still exists as a depot for Virgin Pendolino trains on the Wolverhampton – Birmingham – Euston service and while the Low Level station building remains it serves no railway function. The S&BR of course remains as the route to Shrewsbury.

The LMS lines were electrified in 1967, at which time use of the GWR route for through services to Paddington ceased. The line subsequently closed and was lifted, although from Stow Heath now provides the basis of the Midland Metro route to Birmingham Snow Hill.

This book is an assembly of photographs in colour to create a pictorial tour, mainly from the 1960's to the early years of the present century, of the various lines within Wolverhampton's city boundaries and extending a mile or so beyond to the northwest. It is far from exhaustive but aims to give a reasonably rounded picture of the lines, establishments and motive power existing before the turn of the 20th Century, many now consigned to history. Reference to the accompanying map should assist in locating the various lines and installations included.

Proceeds from the sale of the book will go towards the project for the overhaul of GWR "Manor" 4-6-0 7819 "Hinton Manor" to restore it to active use.

Thanks are due to the following (in no particular order) who have made their photographs available or provided assistance, much appreciated by the author :-

Brian Robbins, Pete Stamper, Doug Nicholson, Ned Williams, David Hayes, John Dew, John Bucknall, David Postle, Kidderminster Railway Museum, Richard Icke, Roger Cromblehome, Michael Mensing, Hugh Ballantyne, Alan Davies, Alan Gough, Colin Gall, David Rowley, Peter Share, Mervyn Srodzinsky, Martin Bonnor, Bob Yate and my wife Christine.

Ned Williams also made available various slides of the late Michael Hale and Pete Stamper those of the late Stan Cartwright.

Simon Dewey, Tettenhall, Wolverhampton, 2010

LOW LEVEL STATION: Wolverhampton Low Level station frontage seen in early 1979. By this time the station was in use as a parcels concentration depot, all passenger use having finally ceased in March 1972. The building retains its protective canopies in the photograph but these were subsequently removed. The station was built during the early 1850's, opening for use on 1st July 1854 for OWWR trains and on 14th November that year for GWR services. In 1984 the building was Listed Grade II and in 1985, following acquisition by Wolverhampton Council, works commenced on its restoration, sadly subsequently abandoned. Following this the station's future fell into limbo until 2007 when restoration recommenced, although even this, at the time of writing, has stalled and awaits completion and the building being brought back to use.
Simon Dewey

September 9th 1962 with the pioneer "King" class 4-6-0 6000 "King George V" running in to the Low Level Up Main platform for its 10.17 a.m. scheduled departure on British Railways' "Farewell to the Kings" special train from Wolverhampton to Swindon. A train of such seminal importance today would see the platforms crammed but evidently not so in 1962! The locomotive had spent the previous week at Stafford Road shed being specially cleaned and prepared for the working and when seen two days before literally smelt of polish. *Michael Hale*

Viewed from Sun Street bridge (now removed), in July 1984 looking north, the station is seen in its final condition as a railway establishment, its use as a parcels concentration depot having ceased in June 1981. By this time the only rail access was via the former Midland Railway connection at Heath Town Junction, trackwork beyond the centre of the station having been lifted as well as from the southern bay platforms each side, that on the Down side being infilled.

When built, the station had an all-over roof but this was removed by the early 1930's although the lofty blue brick walls previously supporting it remained and can be seen in the photograph. Class 25 25 067 stands at the Down main platform with a short train, the whole ensemble forming a mobile exhibition that had earlier been on show at the High Level Station but was removed for temporary storage at Low Level.

Simon Dewey

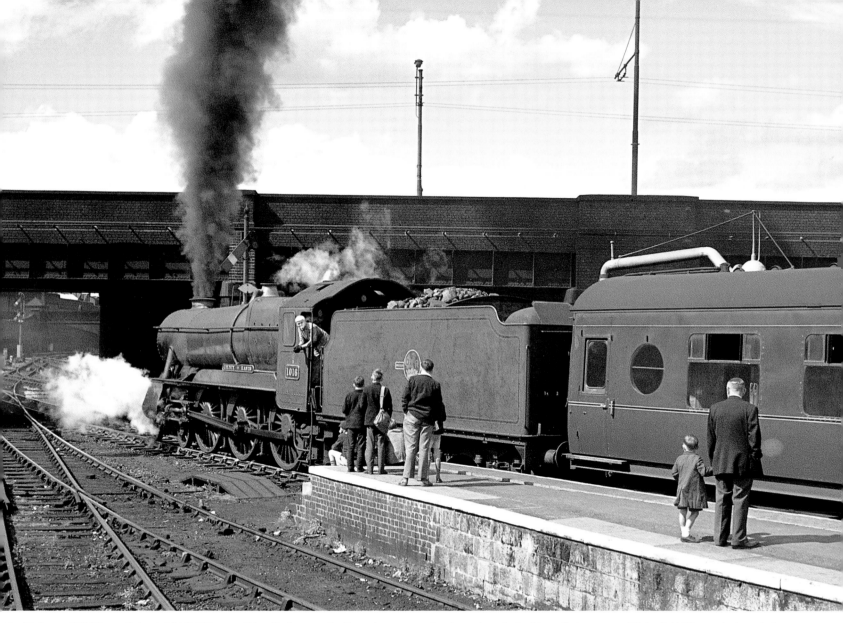

On 4th August 1962 "County " class 4-6-0 1016 "County of Hants", a long-standing Shrewsbury engine, is seen getting to grips with the 09.40 Bournemouth Central to Birkenhead train as it pulls away from the station to pass beneath Wednesfield Road bridge, at that time still sporting the wires and standards of the trolleybus route to Wednesfield. BR steam had exactly 6 years to run but 1016's working life would end sooner, on 17th September 1963. For its first 5½ years the engine had been based at Stafford Road.

Michael Mensing

From 8th September 1962 Wolverhampton gained one named train but also lost one. As from that day the "Cornishman", which from 1952 had started from Low Level on its journey to Penzance, was transferred to run from Sheffield via the MR route to New Street. At the same time the "Pines Express" from Manchester to Bournemouth was rerouted away from its historical route via Birmingham New Street and the Somerset & Dorset line to the Low Level, Snow Hill and the GWR route to Oxford, Reading and Basingstoke. Engines on the "Pines" were changed at Low Level, usually a Stafford Road "Castle" taking the train forward to Oxford. Scheduled to depart at 12.05, an unidentified "Castle" is seen blasting clear of Sun Street bridge with the southbound "Pines" during the summer of 1963. The lines leaving the bottom right of the picture are those up to the Midland Railway at Heath Town Junction. *Stan Cartwright/Pete Stamper collection*

Seen from the opposite side of the tracks from the previous photograph, preserved 45xx Class 2-6-2T No 4555 emerges from the northern end of the tunnel towards Low Level station with a Stephenson Locomotive Society special train touring branch lines in the West Midlands on 13th June 1964. The train had travelled to Wolverhampton from Birmingham Snow Hill via Old Hill and Dudley and would proceed to Stourbridge Junction travelling along the Oxley Branch. Before returning to Birmingham the trip also journeyed to Worcester and Bromyard. The fare was 18/6d (93 pence). The first 20 engines of the same class as 4555 (Nos 4500 to 4519), were the last locomotives built new at Stafford Road Works, between October 1906 and April 1908. The last of these to remain in service was 4507, withdrawn in October 1963. On the bridge above the tunnel portal and across the width of the background is the line from High Level Station to Heath Town Junction, thence via the Midland Railway route to Walsall and the LNWR spur down to the "Old Line" at Portobello Junction. *John Bucknall*

HIGH LEVEL STATION: The main frontage of the original High Level station, built by the LNWR, opened in December 1851 and originally known as Queen Street station , seen in 1961. The old station was demolished and replaced with the present buildings progressively between 1964 and 1967 as part of the electrification and modernisation of the West Coast route from Euston. The ornate elegance of the old building contrasts with the starkness of its replacement. The Queens Building nearby, now incorporated into the present bus station, was originally the entrance to the station approach from the bottom of Queen Street, built using the same brick as the station and complementary architectural detailing. Daytrips to Liverpool on Sundays for 14/- (70p) and a football supporters' special to Manchester for the Football League Division 1 Wolves match against Manchester United on Saturday 30th September for 13/- (65p) are advertised on the main hoardings. Wolves won the match 2-0 but despite being League Champion runners-up and winning the FA Cup in the previous season, at the end of the 1961-2 season they could only achieve 18th position in Division 1, with Manchester United's fortunes little better at 15th .

Stan Cartwright/Pete Stamper collection

The present station can perhaps be most favourably described as functional compared with its predecessor with its Victorian buildings and all-over roof. The view from the North end of Platform 2 in June 1985 with Class 47 47 617 "University of Stirling", well away from its home base of Inverness, awaiting departure northwards from Platform 1. A BR Derby Class 116 DMU has arrived at Platform 2 from Shrewsbury while Class 304 EMU 304 004 stands parked in the middle road, its destination blind reading 'Altrincham'. The middle road has since been removed and the station expanded by provision of a new platform (Platform 4) off to the left of the photograph.

Simon Dewey

11

Seen from the other end of the station, a visiting football supporters' special train formed of the two previous "Midland Pullman" 5-car diesel units has arrived at Platform 2, the western side of the island platforms 2 and 3, in the late 1960's. By this time the units had been transferred to the Western Region to join their longer (8-car) counterparts that had formed the Bristol and Birmingham Pullman trains. The "Birmingham Pullman" was introduced on the Wolverhampton to Paddington route in 1960, being serviced at Cannock Road sidings, leaving Low Level each weekday morning at 7.00 a.m. and returning (following a return trip to Birmingham during the day) at 7.15 p.m.. The service lasted until cessation of through workings to Paddington in March 1967 when the set was transferred away for use on the "South Wales Pullman". The new platform 4 now occupies the site seen on the right of the picture. The collision-damaged nose of the unit round the built-in tail light is noteworthy. Along with all its counterparts the unit was withdrawn in May 1973.

Stan Cartwright/Pete Stamper collection

"Britannia" Pacific 70012 "John of Gaunt" is seen approaching High Level station from the north with the empty stock of a Euston express in 1963. Beyond the front of the engine can be glimpsed the station's overall roof which would be removed during the rebuilding of the station which commenced the following year in preparation for electrification of the line. The date of the roof's actual removal was 22nd February 1965 when the station was necessarily closed for the day while the structure was cut into sections and dropped onto the tracks and platforms for carting away. Wolverhampton No 3 signal box is just visible on the right, one of four manual signal boxes controlling traffic through the High Level lines before being replaced by the present power box, commissioned in August 1965.

John Bucknall

Looking from about the same viewpoint of the photographer of the previous shot, Rugby shed's Black 5 45130 is seen leaving High Level station on an express to Manchester in April 1963, passing a Metro-Cammell 2-car DMU (later Class 101/102) smart in its fresh lined green livery. Diesel multiple units were introduced on local London Midland Region passenger services in the Birmingham area in 1956 and had become widespread in the Wolverhampton area by 1958. 45130 was built by W.G.Armstrong-Whitworth for the LMS in May 1935, lasting in service until January 1967.

Simon Dewey

NORTH OF HIGH LEVEL: The canal lies to the left of the picture behind Wolverhampton No 4 signal box as LMS "Coronation" class Pacific 46245 "City of London" draws the empty stock of a train for Euston out of the carriage sidings up to High Level station in 1963. By this time these top link locomotives had been displaced from their historic Anglo-Scottish express duties by the advance of dieselisation and examples of the class became quite commonplace on Euston to Wolverhampton trains. 46245 was withdrawn in October 1964, returning to the Black Country one last time for breaking up at Cashmore's in Great Bridge 2 months later.

Michael Hale

About a quarter of a mile north of High Level (now Wolverhampton) station the railway crosses the BCN canal on a skew bridge as the line approaches Wolverhampton North Junction. Lock No 3 of the 21 locks on the BCN between Broad Street Basin in Wolverhampton and Aldersley Junction where it meets the Staffs. & Worcester Canal is seen on the right with No 2 beyond, as a summer Saturday working to Pwllheli hauled by a pair of Class 31's both in Dutch grey livery approaches the bridge in 1992. Not visible in the picture, obscured by the trees on the right, is the location of the GWR's large goods depot at Victoria Basin, canal access to which was from what is now Broad Street Basin, at the top of the flight of locks.

Simon Dewey

Lock No 3 forms the foreground as Class 47 47491 "Horwich Enterprise" crosses the skew bridge over the canal heading towards Wolverhampton station with a train from the north in May 1987.

Simon Dewey

Wolverhampton North Junction, where the S&BR line from Oxley Viaduct and Stafford Road Junction meets the SVR line up from Bushbury, as a Class 25 diesel approaches heading for Wolverhampton station with a train of empty stock from Oxley carriage sidings in 1983. The original junction was severed in the 1850's, the two lines running parallel to each other for a short distance with the S&BR line then serving the large goods depot at Victoria Basin, later known as Herbert Street Goods. This was originally built in 1854 and enlarged over the years before being rebuilt in 1930 and is currently in use as Carver's builders' merchants' warehouse. In preparation for closure of the line north from the Low Level station to Cannock Road Junction, the junction was reinstated in 1966. The remnants of the line into Herbert Street Depot can be seen on the left. The SVR line north towards Stafford is seen to the right curving round to cross the Stour Valley viaduct dropping towards Bushbury, seen in the distance with Goodyear's tyre factory visible above it. *Simon Dewey*

The Stour Valley viaduct crossing the Smestow valley, seen from Lock No 14 of the 21 Locks of the BCN between Broad Street and Aldersley on 20th April 2002 with LNER A3 Pacific 4472 "Flying Scotsman" crossing towards the Bushbury end with a VSOE Pullman train from London Victoria to Crewe. The viaduct dates from the 1840's, being built of blue brick with 22 arches, crossing at its immediate southern end in successive arches the canal, the GWR line from Stafford Road Junction and the lines into Stafford Road shed yard. The metal bridge over the canal for the GWR lines is visible below the third coach of the train.

Brian Robbins

The extensive site of Wolverhampton Gasworks flanked the Stour Valley viaduct with, on its eastern edge, the OWWR spur down from Cannock Road Junction to Bushbury Junction, itself flanked by carriage sidings at its southern end. The sidings and Gasworks have gone other than two large gasometers storing natural gas. The OWWR spur is now part of the Bushbury Chord line created to obviate the need for reversing coal trains serving Ironbridge power station at Cannock Road when running between Bushbury and Stafford Road Junctions (as described later in the book). Before formation of the Chord, a Class 47 is seen hauling a loaded coal train along the OWWR line backed by the gasometers, towards Cannock Road Junction in the early 1970's. Although officially the GWR's Bushbury Branch, the spur was known locally as the "Royal Spur", the name deriving from use of the line by Queen Victoria's royal train when travelling between Windsor and Scotland. The SVR viaduct is visible in the background.

Simon Dewey

Wolverhampton Gas Works had its own internal railway system which was served by small 0-4-0 saddle tank locomotives based on site. In the latter days of the works' railway operation the resident locomotives were "Carbon" built by W.G. Bagnall of Stafford in 1902, rebuilt in 1943 and "Victory", another Bagnall-built engine but dating from 1942. These were joined in 1963 by "George Le B Diamond", a Robert Stephenson & Hawthorn-built locomotive transferred from Dudley Port gas works and effectively replacing the two others, which fell into disuse and were subsequently broken up in 1965, finding no purchasers when put up for sale for £50 each. The two older engines are seen at the gasworks in 1963: *Upper* "Carbon" in the heart of the works and *Lower* "Victory" stored almost beneath the SVR viaduct.

Both Stan Cartwright/Pete Stamper collection

OXLEY CHORD: In 1983 a new loop was created from where the GWR line between Stafford Road and Cannock Road Junctions crossed the canal east of Dunstall Park and the SVR viaduct, round to the OWWR line passing alongside the gasworks on its way to the GJR line at Bushbury Junction. Known as the Oxley Chord, it opened for use on 9th August 1983 bringing to an end the reversing arrangements at the old Cannock Road Junction. It is used predominantly by coal trains to and from Ironbridge power station at Buildwas via the S&BR line through Codsall to Lightmoor Junction at Telford but in addition the chord sees occasional use by other workings including empty coaching stock to and from Oxley Sidings. One weekend in May 1983 the line was put to much use by passenger trains diverted via the chord between Stafford Road Junction and High Level while the bridge carrying the S&BR line over the Stafford Road was replaced as part of a road widening scheme. Prevented from heading straight up to Wolverhampton station a Class 47 on a Shrewsbury to Euston train is seen making its way round the chord on its way towards Bushbury. A replacement locomotive will then come onto the rear of the train (by then the front!) to head back over the SVR viaduct up to the station. Oxley viaduct is visible through the arch above the frontward end of the 47.

Simon Dewey

Looking Right from a little above the location of the previous photograph another less typical working, in fact the first passenger working round the Chord (a railtour hauled by the pioneer Class 40 locomotive 40 122, at that time restored to its earlier green livery and number D200) is seen heading round from the Bushbury end on a snowy 16th February 1985. Park Lane bus depot with the Grand Junction line passing in front is visible in the background.

Brian Robbins

DUNSTALL PARK: The Gas Works dominate the scene to the right of the picture as LNWR "Super D" 0-8-0 49361 heads through Dunstall Park station returning from Oxley Sidings on an SLS special train touring the lines of South Staffordshire on 22nd June 1963. Dunstall Park station was opened by the GWR in 1896 and closed by BR in 1968 when all passenger traffic on the route between Low Level and Stafford Road Junction ceased. In its heyday Dunstall Park was much used in connection with horse race meetings at the nearby racecourse and a separate platform for the loading and unloading of horses existed just beyond the station on the Up side, accessible from Gorsebrook Road. The station's Down platform is on the left of the picture, behind the rear wall of which lay the yard of Stafford Road engine shed.

Doug Nicholson

STAFFORD ROAD SHED: The distinctive Victorian framework of the gasometer seen in the previous photograph lies in the background of a view of GW Large Prairie tank 6125, recently outshopped from Stafford Road Works and running-in on Wolverhampton local workings before returning to its home shed at Southall, standing in Stafford Road shed yard in 1960. The

61xx tanks, totalling 70 in number, were a development of Churchward's 51xx engines, with increased boiler pressure, introduced in 1931 to work on the GWR's London area suburban services and until their final years were almost exclusively allocated to Old Oak Common, Slough, Southall, Reading, Didcot and Oxford sheds. *John Bucknall*

A view from the end of the Stour Valley viaduct of Stafford Road shed yard on 8th September 1963, a few days after the shed's closure with the only locomotives present, a "King", 6012 "King Edward VI" and a "Hall", 5910 "Park Hall", both withdrawn, on the line to the right. The shed's active allocation had been transferred to Oxley. The 1930's Repair Shop of Stafford Road Works with its three gable ends dominates the right hand skyline with, visible in front of it (with the factory chimney to its left and water tank to its right) the upper part of the Works' offices. The hipped-ended roofed building in the middle right was the erecting shop of the 1875 arrangement of the Works. The buildings visible on the left are, respectively from left to right, the edge of the three roundhouses dating from 1860 that had formed the shed in its heyday (only one being in use during its latter years, however, housing the depot's smaller tank engines), the "Arcade" (a 2-road straight shed) and the main straight road shed which had 4 roads, starting life in 1854 as a Broad Gauge locomotive shed then being used as the Tender Shop of the Works before reverting to use to house locomotives but by then of standard gauge.

Michael Hale

The straight road shed on the morning of 24th August 1963, only 2 weeks before closure, with "Castles" 7001 "Sir James Milne" and 5026 "Criccieth Castle" awaiting their day's work. Stafford Road was coded SRD in GWR days and 84A under British Railways, being the principal of the Wolverhampton Division sheds. When built it had been home to goods, passenger and shunting engines but following the opening of Oxley shed in 1907 its allocation was predominantly passenger and shunting locomotives only.

Hugh Ballantyne

A comparison in LMS and GWR top link locomotive styles seen in the shed yard : -

Upper: On 22nd June 1963, a little less than three months before the shed's closure, is an exotic visitor in the form of the penultimate Stanier Pacific 46256 "Sir William A. Stanier F.R.S.". Despite its West Coast main line express pedigree the working that had brought the Pacific into Wolverhampton was no more than a pigeon fanciers' special train, a lowly duty for such an engine, indicative of the surrender of the top link steam locomotives to the advance of diesel traction. The SVR viaduct is visible in the right background.   *Doug Nicholson*

Lower: Seen a couple of years earlier is one of Stafford Road's own locomotives, "King" class 6011 "King James I" in sparkling condition ready to leave to run up to Low Level station to take forward an express to Paddington. Built in April 1928, 6011 was based at Stafford Road continuously from January 1946 until September 1962 when transferred to Old Oak Common for 3 months before withdrawal on 18th December of that year, having run a total of 1,718,295 miles during its life.   *John Bucknall*

Stafford Road shed's coaling stage and turntable lay remote from the shed yard beyond the canal, at the end of Fox's Lane, turned and refuelled locomotives leaving to go on shed then crossing the canal on the bridge occupying the foreground of the photograph before passing below the SVR viaduct, the vantage point of the photographer. Class 47 47 344 on a loaded MGR coal train to Ironbridge Power Station is seen on 13th May 1983 accelerating its train away from Cannock Road Junction round past the site of the coaling stage. "The Birdcage", as the location was known, where a pedestrian footpath fenced off from the canal towpath passed through a tunnel under the railway, was a popular haunt of trainspotters, where trains on both the Low Level and High Level lines could be seen as well as locomotive movements on and off Stafford Road shed. Heath Town church spire, near the site of Wolverhampton's first station at Wednesfield Heath, is visible in the centre of the distant skyline. *Brian Robbins*

Locomotives coming onto Stafford Road shed queue up to use the turntable, water column and coaler on the busy summer Saturday afternoon of 29th July 1961. Stafford Road's own 7026 "Tenby Castle" is being coaled, using the primitive manual method typical of GWR sheds, unlike the mechanical system used at Bushbury. Following in line is "Hall" 4921 "Eaton Hall" of Oxford shed, with two GWR Moguls approaching the turntable beyond.

On summer Saturdays, particularly during the industrial fortnight, the local sheds would often be emptied of most of their passenger and mixed traffic engines as these were pressed into service to haul the many extra trains put on to transport Wulfrunians away on holiday. Later in the day as the trains returned home, lines of locomotives would accumulate at the sheds as they awaited servicing.

Michael Mensing

GW "County" Class 1024 "County of Pembroke", then of Bristol St Philip's Marsh shed, alongside the western side of the coaling stage favoured by arriving locomotives, in early 1963, turned and awaiting coaling. When new, 1024 was allocated to Stafford Road itself where it remained for almost 4 years before being transferred to Shrewsbury in 1950. After a life of 17 years and travelling 643,975 miles 1024 was withdrawn in April 1964.

Doug Nicholson

CANNOCK ROAD JUNCTION: Stafford Road's coaling stage can be seen in the distance (to the right of the signals above the second coach of the train) in this view from Cannock Road bridge one Sunday in 1965 as a train from Stoke-on-Trent to Birmingham formed of two 3-car Birmingham RC&W DMU's passes Cannock Road Junction off the OWWR line through Cannock Road sidings (the GWR's Bushbury Branch). Usually routed via the Stour Valley line to New Street, the train had been diverted via the GWR route between Wolverhampton and Birmingham Snow Hill while the SVR was closed for engineering works during electrification of the line. The train will have joined the OWWR line at its junction with the GJR at Bushbury, this junction originally being known as Show Hill Junction but now Bushbury South Junction.

Michael Mensing

Just North of the previous photograph with Cannock Road carriage sidings forming the background and Southern Region coaching stock much in evidence, work is in progress on rerailing "King" 6012 "King Edward VI" which has come to grief straddling two lines at the approach to the sidings on 30th July 1961. Details of the mishap are unknown but the locomotive's tender and cab roof projection have been removed probably in readiness for its being lifted by crane back onto the track in what must have been a difficult operation for the Stafford Road breakdown gang

Richard Icke

Cannock Road Junction lay about ½ mile north of Low Level, where the GWR-built line round to, originally, their broad gauge engine shed at Stafford Road (subsequently extended to connect to the S&BR just south of Oxley viaduct) branched off the OWWR line proceeding to its connection with the GJR at Bushbury. While the line south of the Cannock Road bridge was lifted following cessation of through workings north of Low Level in 1968, the junction survived, although in a rationalised form, to facilitate Merry-Go-Round (MGR) coal trains to Ironbridge power station from collieries north of Wolverhampton (travelling via the GJR through Penkridge and joining the OWWR line at Bushbury South Junction) reversing at Cannock Road before proceeding back north to Madeley Junction via the S&BR. Buildwas-bound trains would stop short of Cannock Road and the locomotive run round to the rear of the train which it would then propel up clear of the junction before setting off in the opposite direction round the GWR line through Dunstall Park and Stafford Road Junction onto the S&BR. Empty trains did a similar manoeuvre in the opposite direction, the whole train running up below Cannock Road bridge and reversing back onto the line to Bushbury, the locomotive then running to the Bushbury end of the train before heading back northwards.

Above: Loaded and empty MGR workings, each in the hands of a Class 47 locomotive, meet at Cannock Road on 6th March 1983 with 47 302 seen pushing its loaded train up to pass below Cannock Road bridge in the distance before setting forwards past 47 298 and its waiting empty train. *Brian Robbins*

Looking north from the same vantage point, the locomotive of a train of empty hoppers returning from Buildwas is seen in the distance about to drop back onto its train before heading past the gasometers towards Bushbury. The line from Stafford Road Junction curves round from the left having passed below the SVR viaduct seen in the background. Goodyear's tyre factory at Bushbury is seen beyond the end of the viaduct and the land between the two routes was the site of part of Cannock Road carriage sidings.

Simon Dewey

PORTOBELLO JUNCTION: Portobello Junction lies just north of Neachells Lane off the Willenhall Road about a mile east of the city centre where the spur built in 1881 up to Heath Town Junction and High Level branches off the original GJR route bypassing the town of the 1830's. Looking north, the 1881 line is seen to the left as the thrysistor-controlled Class 87, 87 101 "Stephenson" is seen passing with a southbound container train along the "Old Line" as the GJR is known locally, in about 1985. This same spot was, on the foggy early morning of 19th October 1899, the scene of a fatal collision between a LNWR freight train heading along the Old Line from Bushbury when it was crashed into by an express down the spur from High Level, killing the crew of the freight train's engine, both Bushbury men.

David Hayes

Taking the spur up to Heath Town Junction away from Portobello and illuminated by the evening sun is a special working from Tyseley to Wolverhampton double-headed by GWR 0-6-0 PT's 7760 and 9600 in the summer of 2000. Neachells Lane bridge lies in the background with Noose Lane level crossing beyond, the site of a station from 1854 to 1873.   *Simon Dewey*

HEATH TOWN TUNNEL: The Old Line north of Portobello enters a lengthy cutting, passing through a tunnel at Heath Town below the Wyrley & Essington canal, the Wednesfield Road and the Midland Railway line from Heath Town Junction towards Wednesfield which itself crossed the canal at the same point, the bridge abutments of which, now removed, are visible in the top Left. A Class 87-hauled express diverted via the GJR during weekend engineering works on the Trent Valley main line emerges from the tunnel's southern portal in 1983. The site of Wolverhampton's first railway station, at Wednesfield Heath, lay about 200 yards beyond the northern end of the tunnel.

Simon Dewey

BUSHBURY: Bushbury Junction, where the SVR line down from High Level meets the GJR, seen from Bushbury Lane bridge as Black 5 4-6-0 44910 sweeps round off the SVR past Bushbury No 1 signal box in 1964, by which time erection of catenary posts for electrification of the route had commenced. The Old Line diverges to the left. The LNWR's Bushbury station, opened in 1852 and closed in 1912, existed here but no traces of it remain. The West Midlands Local Transport plan of 2000 recommended that a study be made into reopening a station at Bushbury although any new station is likely to be sited well north of the original, probably nearer Fordhouses.

Michael Mensing

Looking again from Bushbury Lane bridge but northwards this time, with English Electric Type 4 (subsequently Class 40) No D326 on an Up express signalled for the Stour Valley line in 1964. The lines forming Bushbury Down goods yard lie to the left with Goodyear's tyre factory beyond. To the Right, just off picture is Bushbury engine shed.

The goods yard has now gone, as have the Goodyear's factory buildings seen here, the whole of the background to the picture at the time of writing being a cleared site. D326 had achieved dubious notoriety the previous year as the locomotive involved in the Great Train Robbery.

Michael Mensing

Bushbury engine shed lay to the east of the running lines immediately north of Bushbury Lane bridge, built by the LNWR in about 1860 replacing an older facility 350 yards north of the High Level station (which was subsequently used, with later enlargement, as a carriage shed until the early 1960's). The original Bushbury shed was a timber structure housing about a dozen locomotives. In 1883 a much larger, brick-built shed was constructed in its place. This was reroofed in the late 1950's and lasted until closure in 1965. The shed's allocation until its final years was always a mixture of passenger, freight and shunting classes. Under the LNWR and LMS until 1935 the shed's code was 13. Subsequent to 1935 and into BR days until 1960 it was 3B, then 21C until 1963 and finally 2K. Following closure, the shed's remaining allocation was transferred to Oxley. Sadly not the finest photograph but the scene inside the shed a few weeks before closure with Stanier 2-6-0 42983, a Black 5 and a 2-6-4 tank resting between workings.

Doug Nicholson

41

One of Bushbury's own stud of locomotives at the time, Black 5 4-6-0 44829 stands by the ash disposal tower in the shed yard after coaling in May 1963. 44829 was built at Crewe in August 1944 and lasted until within 3 months of the end of BR steam, being withdrawn in May 1968. It was one of five members of the class converted to oil–burning in 1946 during the coal crisis after the Second World War, being converted back to coal-burning in August 1948.

Simon Dewey

Upper: Rebuilt "Patriot" 4-6-0 45526 "Morecambe and Heysham" outside the front of the shed in 1963. The mechanical coaler can be seen beyond the rear of the locomotive's tender and the upper part of the ash disposal tower is visible above the firebox. *Simon Dewey*

Lower: The shed's allocation in LMS and BR days included a number of veteran Midland Railway 2F 0-6-0's. In unfortunately again not the finest photograph, one such, 58169, a visitor from Bescot shed, is seen resting outside the shed in about 1960. One of the last survivors of the class, the veteran engine, built in 1876, was not withdrawn until February 1961. Sister engine 58148, transferred to Bushbury during 1959 from Burton, lasted even longer, not being withdrawn until December 1963. The shed building's roof was renewed to that shown from its original Northlight form during the late 1950's.
Stan Cartwright/Pete Stamper collection

Mainstay of the latter day LNWR heavy freight locomotive fleet were the 0-8-0's of Classes G1, G2 and G2A dating originally from 1892. Bushbury naturally had an allocation of them throughout their lives, the last examples running locally until as late as 1964 although by that time none were based at Bushbury. G2A 49173 stands in Bushbury goods yard on 24th August 1963.   *Hugh Ballantyne*

Preserved LMS "Jubilee" 4-6-0 No 5690 "Leander" heads north past the site of Bushbury yard on a special working carrying the "Irish Mail" headboard in the summer of 2006 with Goodyear's tyre factory chimney then prominent in the background. The goods yard was closed in the mid 1960's and the track subsequently lifted and even the blue chimney with its yellow GOODYEARS and winged shoe trademark is now a thing of the past, being demolished in 2008 preparatory to redevelopment of the bulk of the previous factory site. From 1939 until early 1960 Bushbury shed was continuously home to an allocation of "Jubilees" for working the Wolverhampton High Level to Euston expresses on which they gained a high reputation in the hands of their Wolverhampton crews.

Simon Dewey

CODSALL: Codsall station on the S&BR, opened in 1849 and still in active use, with Black 5 4-6-0 45004 speeding through on an express to Shrewsbury, Chester and Birkenhead in 1966. By that time LMS and BR classes had supplanted most of the GWR types native to the line. The Up platform Waiting Room has since been reduced in size, shorn of its canopy and pitched roof and the main station building is now a public house. The GWR footbridge dating from 1883, a Listed structure, was accidently demolished during engineering works in June 2005 but has since been restored to its original state at the (correct) insistence of the local Conservation Officer. Five of the bridge's eight cast iron columns had been damaged beyond repair in the incident and new ones were cast at a Wolverhampton foundry.

Brian Robbins

Brush Type 4, Class 47 47 567 "Red Star" heading past Codsall signal box with the 11.40 Shrewsbury to Euston express on 26th September 1985. The station is visible in the background. A goods loop previously existed to the Up side of the main running lines, hence the position of the box set back from the line. The Diesel locomotive will come off the train at the High Level station to be replaced by electric traction onward to Euston. Through services from Shrewsbury to Euston ceased in 1993 although direct London services have recently been revived by the Wrexham & Shropshire Railway, running to Marylebone. Semaphore signalling of the line ceased in 2007, when the box was removed but is understood to have been rescued for preservation.

Brian Robbins

Looking north from Histons Hill bridge, BR Standard Class 5 4-6-0 73025 of Shrewsbury shed heads a mineral train south towards Wolverhampton in 1965. The Up Goods Loop and Down Refuge Siding on their respective sides of the main lines are still intact although the Down siding rails are disused and rusty, the goods yard at Codsall having closed on 7th September 1964. 73025 was built in November 1951 and withdrawn in October 1967 from Patricroft shed where most of the surviving members of the class had graduated by that time. For most of its life, however, 73025 was no stranger to Wolverhampton being variously shedded at Shrewsbury, Chester and Oxley between 1953 and 1965.

Brian Robbins

BILBROOK: Bilbook station, barely a mile south of that at Codsall was originally the GWR's "Birches and Bilbrook Halt" opened in 1934 and is unusual in having its Up and Down platforms staggered and remote from each other, south and north respectively of the Codsall Road crossing Birches Bridge. The name was progressively shortened to "Bilbrook" only when "Halt" was dropped in 1968 followed by the "Birches" reference in 1974.

Upper: A southbound stopping train from Shrewsbury formed of two Metro-Cammell 2-car DMU's approaches Birches Bridge and the Up platform beyond, passing the Down platform in about 1979. The platform is seen at its original length, being subsequently lengthened (towards the bridge) and reformed during the 1980's. Histons Hill bridge, from where the previous photograph was taken, is visible in the distance as the line curves towards Codsall.

Lower: Also viewed from the bridge but looking southwards in August 1992, Class 58 58011 is seen heading from the Wolverhampton direction with a loaded coal train to Ironbridge power station past the station's by then similarly lengthened and reformed Up platform. *Both Simon Dewey*

NEAR OXLEY: About 2 miles north of Wolverhampton city centre the line from Shrewsbury crosses the Staffs & Worcester canal near Oxley. BR 9F 2-10-0 92110 is seen crossing the canal on a Stanlow to Albion Gulf oil train in the winter of 1964. The two tracks on the Left are those of the GWR's Wombourn Branch round from Oxley Middle Junction (about 200 yards behind the photographer) to Oxley Branch Junction, about ½ mile distant, near Aldersley Stadium.

John Bucknall

On 12th April 1985 Class 47 47 324 on a loaded MGR coal working to Ironbridge power station ran driverless away from Oxley sidings onto the truncated end of the Wombourn Branch on the bridge over the canal, becoming derailed and the wagons piling up behind the locomotive. Progressively over the succeeding week the wagons were removed, the 47 righted, rerailed and towed away. The photograph shows the scene on the day of the derailment. The gantry below which the wagons are piled up marks the end of the current track formation and the northern limit of electrification of the former GWR lines, used as a headshunt to the carriage washing plant at the present Oxley train care depot.

Simon Dewey

Seen from Aldersley Road, brand new Class 52 "Western" diesel-hydraulic D1047 "Western Lord" stands at the head of a southbound freight from Crewe short of Oxley Branch Junction, having come round the northwestern arm of the triangle of lines between Oxley Branch, North and Middle junctions in February 1963. The "Western" will come off its train, handing over to a "Hall" and work light engine round the opposite arm of the triangle to Oxley shed before onward progression to the Western Region and its first home at Cardiff Canton.   *Doug Nicholson*

LMS 8F 2-8-0 48548 sets off along the single track Wombourn branch from Oxley Branch Junction in April 1963 on the 12 Noon SX freight from Crewe towards Stourbridge Junction where it will arrive (if on time) at 4.45p.m.. Construction of the branch was commenced in 1913 but took 12 years to complete due to the First World War, not opening until 11th January 1925. Passenger services lasted only until 31st October 1932 but the line remained in use as a valuable route for freight trains to bypass the busy Black Country corridor until closure at the end of February 1965.

Simon Dewey

OXLEY SHED: Seen from the Wombourn Branch in the late summer of 1967 with rose bay willow herb prominent in the foreground is the red brick building of Oxley engine shed, closed by this time but still playing host to a breakdown train and carrying out retubing and other repairs to steam locomotives visiting specifically for that purpose. To the immediate Right of the shed can be seen the coaling stage, with (moving further Right) Oxley viaduct and beyond that the bluer brick gables of Stafford Road locomotive works' 1930's-built Repair Shop. *Simon Dewey*

Oxley shed was completed by the GWR in 1907, a Churchward standard 2 turntable unit but due to the narrowness of the site formed with the turntables one behind the other rather than side by side. The shed was some 181 feet wide by 450 feet long (55 x 137 metres approximately) and each turntable of 65 feet (19.75 m approx) diameter with 26 and 24 stabling roads off respectively excluding the access roads. The shed was completely demolished during 1968 apart from the Mess Room block at its southeastern corner, which remains as part of the Alstom West Coast Train Care depot now occupying the site. GW 0-6-0 pannier tanks 9630 and 9610 are seen on 11th September 1966 refuelling at the coaling stage during working an SLS "Farewell to the Panniers" railtour over lines in the West Midlands, the engines having come off the train at Low Level station before adjourning to Oxley to be coaled and watered. Coaling operations at Oxley (as at Stafford Road) were somewhat primitive and wholly carried out by hand, with loaded tubs of coal being wheeled out onto projecting platforms to discharge into the bunker or tender of the locomotive below. In stark contrast, Bushbury shed possessed mechanical coaling facilities. The shed building lies in the background.

Simon Dewey

Standing outside the entrance to the shed's Lifting Shop is 56xx 0-6-2T 5612, recently outshopped from Stafford Road Works and running in before returning to its home shed of Llanelly, in 1960. The main front entrance to the cavernous interior of the shed lay through the central of the three gable end walls, the roof of which is just visible above the engine's safety valve cover. The block on the Right housed the shed's offices and stores.

W. Potter/Kidderminster Railway Museum

Locomotives parked alongside the Western side of Oxley shed

Upper: "Modified Hall" 6971 "Athelhampton Hall" and

Lower: "Britannia" Pacific 70049 "Solway Firth" in the Spring and Summer respectively of 1963.

Although itself a Tyseley engine at the time, the "Hall" is typical of the shed's latter day GWR mixed traffic allocation of 4-6-0's which included "Granges" and "Manors", together with 43xx Moguls, 28xx heavy freight 2-8-0's and the ubiquitous 57xx and 94xx pannier tanks for shunting and local trip workings. Small numbers of 66xx 0-6-2T's and 72xx heavy freight 2-8-2T's also formed part of Oxley's early 1960's complement of ex GWR types. In 1953 a stud of 0-6-0 diesel-electric shunters (now Class 08) was allocated to the shed to replace the pannier tanks shunting the busy Oxley Sidings marshalling yards.

GWR types were displaced by LMS and BR Standard classes during the final years of the shed's life, including, from June to September 1965 principally for use on summer Saturday extras, three "Britannias" although 70049 was not one of them.

Both Simon Dewey

A view inside the shed in July 1964 with "Castle" 5089 "Westminster Abbey" dominating the centre of the picture flanked by 57xx pannier tanks stabled off the frontward of the two turntables, its boarded surface seen in the foreground. 5089 was an Oxley engine at this time, having been transferred from Stafford Road when that shed closed the previous September. It is seen here minus its tender and with its wheel tyres and pistons rusty through lack of use, the engine remaining in this state for several weeks, with withdrawal coming in November after a life of 25 years. Its final journey would be being hauled to Great Bridge for breaking up at Cashmore's. The turntable boarding visible was subsequently removed exposing the pit, although the rearward table remained boarded over until the end of the building's life. Smoke chute hoods intended to capture smoke from engines parked beneath them and funnel it through the roof of the building are prominent at the top of the picture.

John Dew

Parked inside the by now-closed shed in 1967 is a surviving remnant of OWWR No 34, originally an 0-6-0 tender engine dating from 1855, subsequently renumbered 252 after entering GWR service. Following the locomotive's withdrawal in 1904 it was reduced to the form shown and installed at Stafford Road Works for use as a Teaching Frame to instruct enginemen in the workings of a steam locomotive where it was known as "The Model". Operated by a handwheel and with the cylinders cut away to reveal the pistons and valve arrangements, the movements of the various components could be studied with the motion in different positions. It was subsequently housed in a pit in one of the roundhouses at Stafford Road shed. When the shed was demolished the machine was salvaged and propelled to Oxley, for storage pending a decision on its future, unfortunately suffering damage in the process. Neither Clapham Museum nor Wolverhampton Corporation were interested in it and it was eventually taken to the Staffordshire County Museum at Shugborough Hall although never put on public display. It was subsequently removed to the Armley Mills Industrial Museum in Leeds (E.B. Wilson, the builders of the original locomotive being a Leeds firm) where it remains, although dismantled and with its future very uncertain.

J.Tarrant/Kidderminster Railway Museum

Projecting out of the doorway at the northern end of the shed building is "Castle" 5054 "Earl of Ducie" on July 19th 1964. The engine had been one of a group of specially selected members of the class earmarked to haul the steam-hauled high speed special train run two months earlier, in May, to commemorate the exploit in 1904 of "City of Truro" on an Ocean Mails Special when it was the first train recorded to exceed 100 mph (although this is nowadays contested) and retains some of its specially cleaned condition, despite the accumulation of smokebox ash. *John Dew*

The sandstone terrain of the site of Oxley shed can be appreciated from this view looking out through the shed's eastern side doorway in 1963 where "Grange" 4-6-0 6814 " Highnam Grange" is seen awaiting transfer to Stafford Road Works for repair, its connecting rods tied to the engine's handrail above its running plate. On the left is the Sand Hearth, a sideward projection from the main building where sand for use in locomotives' sanders was dried using heat from the shed's two stationary boilers. Two large doorways existed in each side wall of the main shed building but only the frontward one in each case was ever used, the rearward ones being incorporated for access to a further turntable in a future possible extension to the shed as built, but never in the event required.

Simon Dewey

Class 08 diesel shunter 08 901, specially "waterproofed" for operations at Oxley including taking stock through the carriage washing plant, stands on the access throat into and out of Oxley shed yard (by this time a carriage maintenance depot) in June 1986, while a Class 86 electric arrives with stock from a Euston train in the background. The line down from Wolverhampton North Junction over Oxley viaduct and into Oxley Sidings had by this time been electrified but the depot access line remained to be so treated, this not taking place until 1990. The lower quadrant signal controlling exit from the yard still remains in 2010, the last semaphore signal on the working railway in Wolverhampton, still complete with its distinctive GWR finial. The present Oxley signal box, replacing the previous Oxley South and Middle and Stafford Road Junction boxes closed on 30th March 1969, is visible beyond the signal post. At the time of writing this box is scheduled for decommissioning in the near future.

Simon Dewey

OXLEY SIDINGS: Viewed from the present signal box's predecessor, Oxley South Box, Black 4-6-0 45089 is seen setting off southwards on a Class F unfitted express freight out from Oxley sidings in about 1965. Oxley Sidings were Wolverhampton's largest marshalling yard, lying immediately to the north of Oxley viaduct and in their heyday constantly busy. The Down side sidings were split into the Crewe and Birkenhead Yards respectively, totalling 18 sidings and loops , the longest capable of holding 50 wagons. The longer, Up side sidings constituted the Old Yard, Middle Sidings and New Yard, totalling 23 sidings, slot sidings and loops, the longest capable of holding 70 wagons in addition to tender engine and brake van. The running lines from and to Shrewsbury form the two tracks immediately to the left of the locomotive. Oxley Sidings officially closed as a marshalling yard on 3rd October 1967 but while most of the Up side has gone, the Down side remains as part of the present Oxley train care depot

Michael Hale

OXLEY VIADUCT: Completed by 1849 and spanning the Smestow valley between the high ground each side, Oxley viaduct is 188 yards (approximately 171 metres) long and formed in 12 arches, one set to the skew to accommodate the BCN canal passing through, which predates the viaduct by some 77 years. It has the claim to fame of being effectively the furthest point north reached by Brunel's Broad Gauge, although via "mixed" gauge tracks to create a headshunt for trains to and from the goods depot at Victoria Basin via the line between Low Level and Stafford Road Junction. For many years, while Oxley Sidings operated as a freight marshalling yard, an old coach body existed cantilevered out from the viaduct's northern end, used as the "Droppers-in" cabin. The "Droppers-in" sorted goods wagons into their appropriate sidings, the yard being controlled by Oxley South and Middle signal boxes.

Opposite: Two preserved GWR 57xx 0-6-0PT's, 7760 and 9600, are seen crossing the skew arch of the viaduct in August 2000 bringing the empty stock of an evening special train from Tyseley to Wolverhampton into Oxley Sidings before running round their train and returning to Birmingham.

Above: Class 47 47 662 in large logo blue livery is seen crossing southwards in early 1987 on a Shrewsbury to Euston service, changing to electric traction at Wolverhampton station.

Both Simon Dewey

STAFFORD ROAD WORKS: The site of Stafford Road Locomotive Works extended from the southern end of Oxley viaduct each side of the line up to the then Herbert Street Goods depot to where it crossed the Stafford Road and south of the line round to Dunstall Park station, together, originally, with part of the lower level Stafford Road engine shed site to the east of the Stafford Road. The Works developed from a small establishment built by the S&BR on the opening of their line in 1849, expanded by the GWR variously between 1857 and the 1930's. Between 1859 and 1906 794 locomotives were built, together with 6 railmotor units, before new construction ceased following completion of the first 20 locomotives of what became the 45xx class of 2-6-2T's. New construction thereafter became wholly centred on Swindon but Stafford Road remained the GWR's Northern Division locomotive headquarters, continuing with repairs. The earlier buildings being by then too small to deal with the increased size of locomotives of the day, to modernise the facilities the Works were reorganised and a new Erecting Shop was built and brought into use by 1935. Wolverhampton-built locomotives were nothing if not durable: on Nationalisation of the railways in 1948 no fewer than 220 examples dating variously back to 1879, over a quarter of the total built, were taken into BR stock, the last one (2-6-2T 4507 of 1907) surviving until 1963. The Works closed on 1st June 1964, GWR 28xx 2-8-0 2859 being the last locomotive dealt with. It is now preserved and undergoing restoration at the Llangollen Railway.

Opposite: 14xx Class 0-4-2T 1466 is seen on a short train at the edge of the Works complex adjacent to the reception sidings close to Stafford Road Junction on 5th March 1961, a long way from its Devon home, running in after overhaul but only partial repainting. The signal visible above the van next to the engine controls the line approaching the Junction from Dunstall Park. To the right of the engine in the middle distance can be seen the horse platform where rail-borne racehorses visiting Dunstall Park racecourse were unloaded and loaded, beyond which in the far distance is Goodyear's tyre factory, opposite which was Bushbury engine shed. Following withdrawal in December 1963, 1466 became the first locomotive acquired for preservation by the Great Western Society at whose Didcot headquarters it is now based.

John Dew

Above: The reception sidings seen from outside the northern end of the 1935 Repair Shop with a variety of locomotives awaiting entry to the Works for overhaul and repair. The building on the Right is the Inspection Pit House and that on the Left the Engine Weighbridge House. In the foreground are piled discarded firebars from locomotives in the Works for repair.

W.Potter/Kidderminster Railway Museum

Views inside the repair Shop in 1963:

Two GW Large Prairie tanks, the closer, 5152, a Banbury engine, undergoing Heavy Repair in the early stages of reassembly awaiting refitting of its boiler and upper parts. One of its side

tanks, in its green undercoat, can be seen on the floor in the left of the picture. The driving wheels have been remachined and painted but no pistons or connecting rods have yet been fitted. Despite so recent a major repair, the locomotive was withdrawn in November the following year.

J.Tarrant/ Kidderminster Railway Museum

57xx 0-6-0PT 4629, having been fully repainted, approaching completion for release following Heavy Repair. Like Swindon, the Works did not possess a separate paint shop and repainting was carried out within the repair shop itself. Refurbished connecting rods (possibly from 5152) occupy the foreground of the picture and one of the building's four 50 Ton overhead electric travelling cranes can be made out in the top left.

J.Tarrant/ Kidderminster Railway Museum

LOW LEVEL TO MR SPUR, SOUTH OF THE STATION: Immediately south of Sun Street bridge was a spur connecting Low Level to the MR's High Level to Walsall and Sutton Park line via Wednesfield. Stopped half-way up the spur is "Modified Hall" 4-6-0 6964 "Thornbridge Hall" of Shrewsbury shed on a train of mixed empty coaching stock including a BR Mark I Kitchen Car immediately next to the engine, about to set back into the Low Level station carriage shed, in about 1963. Behind the half-mile post can be seen part of the yard of Wednesfield Road Goods depot, with the GWR road motor garage adjacent to the end of Sun Street bridge beyond, seen to the right of the engine's smokebox. *Stan Carpenter/Pete Stamper collection*

WEDNESFIELD ROAD GOOD DEPOT: Wednesfield Road Goods depot was built by the Midland Railway between 1878 and 1881 on a site bounded by Sun Street, Wednesfield Road, Lincoln Street and the railway spur up from Low Level to Heath Town Junction. Rail access was from this last down and round into the depot with road access off Wednesfield Road. Although Listed Grade II following closure in 1988, the building was demolished in 1998 and the site redeveloped for use as Wolverhampton's main postal sorting and delivery offices. Bushbury-shedded Stanier "Crab" 2-6-0 42966 is seen ready to depart from the yard with a train of bogie bolster wagons in the early 1960's. The main warehouse building is seen to the right. A Bristol L-type single deck bus is visible at the WR road motor garage in the upper left of the picture. A reminder of the old depot exists in the form of one of the internal pillar cranes preserved on the forecourt of the new facility.

Stan Carpenter/Pete Stamper collection

LMS LINES SOUTH OF HIGH LEVEL: Where the Stour Valley line from High Level crosses the Bilston Road is the site of a station that had existed at Monmore Green between 1863 and 1916. It is also the location of the junction with the main line of a branch curving round and down to serve the present Wolverhampton Steel Terminal and a previous continuation into the British Oxygen depot. Class 40 40 015 "Aquitania" and a train of liquid oxygen tankers are seen drawing off the connecting line onto the main SVR line just beyond the bridge over Bilston Road in 1982.   *Simon Dewey*

The Steel Terminal site includes the old LNWR Walsall Street canal trans-shipment shed which embodies a basin off the immediately adjacent BCN flanked by railway platforms each side arranged to give level access between boat, platform and road or rail vehicle. Here goods were transferred between railway trucks and canal narrow boats and vice versa. The structure still stands, being Listed Grade II, although is effectively disused for other than storage. Class 58 58 042 in Mainline blue livery stands with a train of bogie wagons loaded with steel bars in about 2000 with the trans-shipment shed beyond.

Ned Williams

GWR LINES SOUTH OF LOW LEVEL: Priestfield, about a mile south of Low Level station, was the point at which the GWR-owned Birmingham Wolverhampton & Dudley Railway line from Birmingham Snow Hill joined the OWWR entering the town from Stourbridge and Dudley (The BW&D did not live up to its name in this respect). The station, just south of the junction itself, had platforms against the face of each of the four lines involved. Looking towards Wolverhampton on 14th April 1962, the scene with

0-6-0PT 3692 taking the OWWR route towards Dudley with the single coach 12.07 train from Low Level. The BW&D route passes out of the picture on the right. Passenger trains between Priestfield and Stourbridge ceased on 30th July 1962. The broad-gauge origin of the site is indicated by the wide formation between the platforms. Edging and paving bricks were rescued from the Stourbridge line platforms when they were dismantled, for re-use on the Severn Valley Railway.   *Michael Hale*

About one mile beyond Priestfield on the OWWR line lay Bilston West station. In what has the deceptive appearance of an almost rural setting, GWR Large Prairie tank 4140 of Stourbridge Junction shed approaches bunker first with the 13.57 stopping train from Low Level to Dudley and Stourbridge made up of three non-corridor suburban coaches on 8th July 1962, barely 3 weeks before the service ceased. Stewart & Lloyds' Spring Vale steelworks lay to the left of the picture, the access to which from the OWWR line lay just short of the station via a line known as Hickmans Branch.

Michael Hale

Spring Vale steelworks was home to an extensive internal railway system, both standard and narrow gauge, worked by steam locomotives until the late 1950's when they were replaced by diesels. Andrew Barclay 0-4-0ST "Victor", a typical example of the latter day steam locomotive fleet, is seen within the steelworks complex shortly before cessation of steam operations. In addition to being connected to the OWWR, the steelworks were also served by the Stour Valley line which passed along the west of the vast site. *Stan Carpenter/Pete Stamper collection*

The GWR (BW&D) route from Priestfield passed principally through cutting to beyond Bilston, skirting Hickman Park about ½ mile beyond Priestfield along the way. The Royal train hauled by "Castle" 4082 "Windsor Castle" is seen heading past Hickman Park towards Wolverhampton carrying the Queen on her visit to Wolverhampton on 24th May 1962. 4082 was really 7013 "Bristol Castle", the two locomotives having exchanged identity in 1952 when the true 4082, the Western Region's Royal engine was required at short notice to haul King George VI's funeral train but was at Worcester awaiting repair and thus unavailable. Instead, its name and number were transferred to 7013, recently outshopped from Swindon, to carry out the duty. The two locomotives never reverted to their original identities.

Michael Hale

Bilston Central station looking south in 1972 not long before cessation of services from Low Level to Birmingham, by that time reduced to only a couple of morning and evening shuttle workings using a single unit diesel railcar, seen approaching from its previous stop at Wednesbury. The station had opened in 1854, at which time the line was laid to "mixed" gauge with both standard and broad (7 feet) gauge tracks as part of Brunel's unfulfilled dream of Broad Gauge to the Mersey, hence the wide gap between the platform faces. The broad gauge got no further north than Oxley. The wide design of the footbridge for a relatively small station is notable. The line now forms the route of the Midland Metro between Wolverhampton and Snow Hill, trams joining the old railway route at Stow Heath.

Roger Cromblehome

"Grange" Class 4-6-0 6863 "Dolhywel Grange" on a Class C express fitted freight in about 1963 heading south near Moxley. St Leonard's church in the centre of Bilston is visible in the background above the last of the train's first group of vans. Oxley shed maintained a stud of "Granges", Collett-designed GWR 2-cylinder mixed traffic locomotives with 5'8" (1428mm) diameter driving wheels, but 6863 at the time was a Reading locomotive.

Michael Hale

This book is one of number of projects by the Wolverhampton Branch of the Severn Valley Railway in support of the fund to restore GWR "Manor" No 7819 "Hinton Manor" to working order and a return to operation on the Severn Valley Railway.

"Hinton Manor" was built at Swindon Works in February 1939 and ran on the GWR and British Railways until its withdrawal from Shrewsbury shed in November 1965, being towed to Barry Island the following year for breaking up. Fortunately this did not occur and 7819 was rescued from the scrapyard and by 1977 had been restored to run on the Severn Valley Railway, operating for many years not only on the SVR but also on several occasions on the main line, until put into storage in 1994 to await major overhaul.

In recent years 7819 has been smartened by a repaint into plain green livery prior to its being placed on show in the MacArthur Glen shopping complex in the town of its birthplace. Here a small dedicated gang of volunteers look after the locomotive's wellbeing.

In preservation 7819 was originally owned by the Hinton Manor Fund with the Wolverhampton Branch of the Severn Valley Railway Association the largest part owner but the locomotive is now in the ownership of the SVR Rolling Stock Trust Company Limited (SVR RST) – Charity Number 1092723 following sale to the Trust for £1.00.

With the locomotive not having run for many years but hoped now to be returned to active use as soon as possible, overhaul is of great importance and the SVR RST's aim in raising money is to enable that work to be carried out to the highest standards of restoration, to match the mechanical standards to which 7819 was built. To this end the RST has already funded the

In a scene that could hopefully be repeated in years to come, "Hinton Manor" is seen near Llangelynin between Tywyn and Llwyngwril on the Cambrian Coast line, hauling a steam special "Cardian Bay Express" from Machynlleth to Barmouth in the summer of 1987.
Alan Davies

acquisition of a complete set of steel tyres for the driving and bogie wheels. There is a long way to go . Overhaul is expected to cost between £300,000 and £400,000. The more that can be raised the sooner this will be achieved.

The SVR Wolverhampton Branch's interest in "Hinton Manor" remains as strong as ever and in support of the RST's efforts have produced this book, the proceeds of sale of which will be devoted to 7819's restoration fund.

In addition the Branch have commissioned a painting by Frederick Lea GRA – "In Cambrian Country" – of the "Hinton Manor" in British Railways' days climbing Talerddig bank on the Cambrian line between Welshpool and Machynlleth on the "Cambrian Coast Express", a train with which the "Manors" became synonymous in the 1950's and 60's. A limited issue of 500 prints of the painting is being produced by the Branch for sale.

The Branch have also commissioned an OO gauge model of GWR "Toad" brakevan No. W 35734, the van allocated specifically to Wolverhampton Stafford Road locomotive department for use when transferring locomotives dead to and from Stafford Road Works for and after repair. This will be available later in the year.

Finally an appeal for colour photographs for a possible further book :-

For what in its time was arguably a "railway" town, albeit not on the scale of Swindon or Crewe, Wolverhampton has tended to be somewhat of a "Cinderella" area for photographic coverage of its railways, particularly in colour and particularly of the LMS lines. It is because of this that a few of the photographs in this book are not of optimum quality but have been included for their particular historical or archive value in the absence of better ones being discovered.

The author would be very pleased to hear from any readers of the book who have any such colour photographs against the possibility of producing a further volume.